# Las hormigas y nosotros

por Mary Nathan

ilustrado por Jason Wolff

Scott Foresman
is an imprint of

PEARSON

Glenview, Illinois • Boston, Massachusetts • Mesa, Arizona
Shoreview, Minnesota • Upper Saddle River, New Jersey

Illustrations by Jason Wolff

ISBN 13: 978-0-328-41096-5
ISBN 10:     0-328-41096-9

**Copyright © Pearson Education, Inc. or its affiliate(s). All Rights Reserved.**
Printed in the United States of America. This publication is protected by copyright and permission should be obtained from the publisher prior to any prohibited reproduction, storage in a retrieval system, or transmission in any form or by any means, electronic, mechanical, photocopying, recording, or likewise. For information regarding permission(s), write to: Pearson School Rights and Permissions, One Lake Street, Upper Saddle River, New Jersey 07458.

Pearson and Scott Foresman are trademarks, in the U.S. and/or other countries, of Pearson Education, Inc. or its affiliate(s).

2 3 4 5 6 7 8 9 10 V010 17 16 15 14 13 12 11 10

Nosotros construimos un hogar.

Las hormigas construyen un hogar.

Nosotros comemos.

Las hormigas comen.

Nosotros trabajamos juntos.

Las hormigas trabajan juntas.